Rio Grande

Photo by Van Beacham

Rio Grande

Craig Martin

Frank Amato
PORTLAND

River Journal

Volume V, Number 1, 1997

At the age of 10, Craig Martin landed his first fish, a four-inch "sunny" from a farm pond near his home in the suburbs of Philadelphia. His next catch was a long time coming: Twenty-three years later he took a wild brown trout on a fly from a headwater of the Rio Grande. He hasn't stopped chasing wild trout since, maintaining a special fondness for exploring small streams in the southern Rockies and San Juan Mountains of New Mexico and Colorado. Craig is an outdoor writer whose works extend beyond fly fishing to hiking, backpacking, cross-country skiing and mountain biking. He lives in Los Alamos, New Mexico — near the rim of White Rock Canyon — with his wife and two children, who share most of his outdoor adventures.

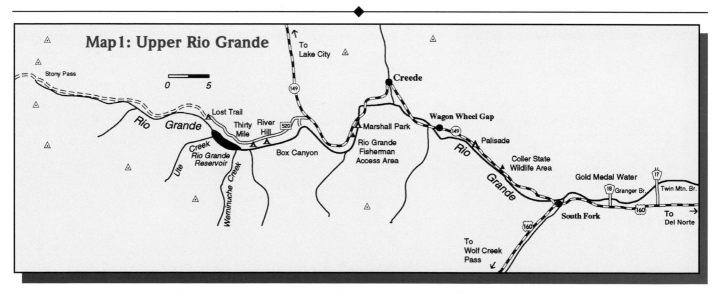

Access to the Rio Grande

Access Point	Location of Trailhead	Hike to River	Access Point	Location of Trailhead	Hike to River
Lobatos Bridge	9 miles east of Antonito, Colorado on paved Kiowa Hill Road	access at river level, downstream only	Big Arsenic Trail	On NM 378, 9 miles west of Cerro in National Wild and Scenic River Recreation Area	1.5 miles, 800 feet on excellent trail
Sunshine Valley Road	28 miles north of Taos, 6 miles west on rough dirt Sunshine Valley Road, then north	.25 mile, 200 feet on primitive route	Little Arsenic Trail	On NM 378, 10 miles west of Cerro in National Wild and Scenic River Recreation Area	1 mile, 800 feet on excellent trail
Lees Trail	28 miles north of Taos, 6 miles west on rough dirt Sunshine Valley Road, then south	.25 mile, 300 feet on good trail	La Junta Trail	On NM 378, 12 miles west of Cerro in National Wild and Scenic River Recreation Area	1 mile, 800 feet on poor trail
Sheep Crossing Trail	On NM 378, 2 miles west of Cerro in National Wild and Scenic River Recreation Area	.5 mile, 300 feet on good trail	El Aguaje Trail	On NM 378, 12 miles west of Cerro in National Wild and Scenic River Recreation Area	2 miles, 800 feet on excellent trail
Chiflo Trail	On NM 378, 3 miles west of Cerro in National Wild and Scenic River Recreation Area	.5 mile, 300 feet on steep trail	Cebolla Mesa Trail	15 miles north of Taos, 4 miles west on fair dirt Forest Road 9	1.5 miles, 900 feet on excellent trail
Bear Crossing	On NM 378, 4 miles west of Cerro in National Wild and Scenic River Recreation Area	1 mile, 500 feet on rugged trail	Garrapata Canyon Trail	14 miles north of Taos, 3 miles west on poor jeep track	1 mile, 400 feet on poor trail

Acknowledgments

Special thanks to Taylor Streit for sharing his more than twenty years of observations on the nature of the Rio Grande; to Van Beacham for passing on his love and infectious enthusiasm for the Gorge; to Tom Knopick for his initiation into the delights of floating the upper river and his patience with my habitual upstream mend; to John Alves of the Colorado Department of Wildlife for his lessons on trout biology; to Chris Duffy for cheerfully creating artworks of feather and fur; and to Kevin Ott for his companionship during past days spent getting to know the river a little better.

Series Editor: Frank Amato—Kim Koch

Subscriptions:
Softbound: $35.00 for one year (four issues)
$65.00 for two years
Hardbound Limited Editions: $95.00 one year,
$170.00 for two years
Frank Amato Publications, Inc. • P. O. Box 82112
Portland, Oregon 97282 • (503) 653-8108

Cover photograph by Kevin Ott
Printed in Hong Kong
Softbound ISBN: 1-57188-089-5
Hardbound ISBN: 1-57188-090-9
(Hardbound Edition Limited to 500 Copies)

© 1997 Frank Amato Publications, Inc.
P. O. Box 82112, Portland, Oregon 97282
(503) 653-8108

Access Point	Location of Trailhead	Hike to River
Cedar Springs Trail	Across John Dunn Bridge and up to west rim, 5 miles north on rough jeep tracks	1 mile, 700 feet on fair trail
San Cristobal Creek	11 miles north of Taos, 3 miles west on poor jeep track	1 mile, 400 feet on primitive route
San Diego Trail	10 miles north of Taos, 2 miles west on rough dirt road	1 mile, 600 feet on poor trail
John Dunn Bridge	8 miles north of Taos, 3 miles west of Arroyo Hondo on good gravel road	river level access upstream and downstream
Manby Hot Springs	7 miles north of Taos, 3 miles west on good dirt road, then 2 miles south on poor dirt tracks	1 mile, 400 feet on good trail
Raven Trail	Across Rio Grande High Bridge, 1 mile north then east on dirt roads	.5 mile, 600 feet on steep trail
Powerline Trail	14 miles south of Taos on NM 68 to NM 578 and west rim, north 4 miles on dirt tracks	1 mile, 700 feet on steep, rough trail
Orilla Verde Recreation Area	14 miles south of Taos on NM 68, 1 mile west of Pilar on paved NM 578	5 miles of river level access parallel to road

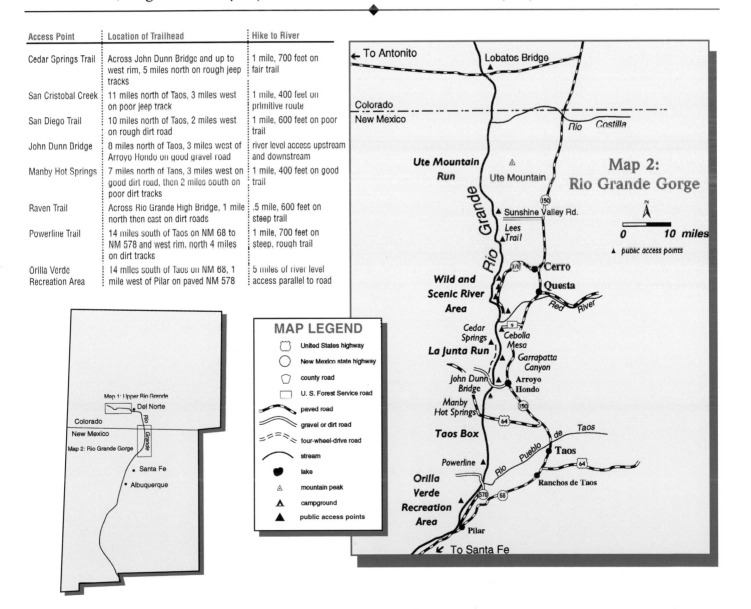

The Rio Grande lies hidden deep within its gorge as a summer thunderstorm rolls over. Photo by S. Brooks Bedwell

Rio Grande

The Mysterious River

Slipping on a chunk of black lava—slick and shiny like a gemstone tumbled in a monstrous lapidary—I danced the Rio Grande Shuffle, a quick two-step designed to keep me upright. With balance restored, I carefully planted my feet and made another cast. As the line unfurled over the water, I checked the forward motion of my arm. The heavily weighted crayfish pattern plopped like a stone into the fast water below a ledge where the entire flow of the river hopped a couple feet toward the level of the sea.

I had cast to such deep runs most of the morning and had only a single 12-inch rainbow-cutthroat hybrid to show for all the effort. After standing in the shadow of the canyon walls since what felt like the beginning of time, the autumn sun finally warmed my back. I was relaxed, giving more than half of my attention to studying the layers of lava and burnt orange soil that made up the canyon wall.

When the fly line jerked to an abrupt stop, my mind quickly returned to fishing and I lifted the rod tip a few inches. Nothing happened, but whatever held the hook was heavy. I figured I'd snagged a drowned cottonwood trunk that slammed downstream during runoff. That's when the alleged log suddenly darted upstream, spinning a bunch of line off the reel as it went.

It was a monumental struggle to keep the fish from wriggling into the cover of the rocks on the far bank. He dove and shook his head more vehemently than my young son refusing his broccoli, then reversed direction and took me downtown, to the foot of the run. Splashing awkwardly through the shallows toward the fish, I finally managed to work him close to the surface. The red spots on his flank confirmed it was a huge brown, the biggest I'd ever laid eyes on.

Seeing so much daylight must have spooked him. He jerked his head downward, and with a snap the line went limp. The champion brown was gone, but my pounding heart felt more than content. It was enough to have seen his shining green sides flash in the current.

It was not an uncommon experience in the Rio Grande Gorge. Angling between the tortured walls of stone requires a lot of effort to find and maybe hook a couple fish. At the end of the day, you'll remember the details of when, where, and how you fought each one. A trip to the Gorge, even if you land no fish, is always satisfying.

We often read in fly fishing literature about where to find trophy trout, and too frequently the modern answer is in artificial trout waters created below dams that resemble prison walls. That's not my vision of the essence of fly fishing. To me the sport is as much about the river as it is tackle, insects and trout. A river isn't

Rugged banks, deep holes, and swift currents mean anglers must meet the Rio Grande on its own terms. The river is a throwback to the untamed streams of years past. Photo by Van Beacham

just where I can find a brown or a rainbow. It is a trout place, a natural cathedral where I can spend time adjusting to the rhythms of nature.

For its entire life as a trout stream, the Rio Grande is such a place. It is a throwback to a different era of fly fishing, where each moment spent angling offers more delights than the opportunity to catch a fish. It is a demanding river, rugged and wild, holding challenging trout that, if you can find them, will chomp your fly, bust the surface with a colossal jump, startle you with the speed with which they swim upstream, then shred your leader on a submerged rock and be gone.

The Rio Grande—simply "Big River" in Spanish— is the unsung giant among American rivers. The second-longest river in the United States, flowing 1,885 miles from headwaters to the sea, is a river of mystery, virtually unknown to the world outside its drainage. What fleeting image the river does have in the consciousness of America is a false impression painted in black and white. Countless double-reel westerns, pumped from Hollywood like slugs from a six-shooter, portrayed dusty cowboys reaching across a parched

plain for a trickle of water they called the Rio Grande. The lower two-thirds of the Rio Grande is indeed such a desert stream. But the top third of the river is another world, one of summer snowfields, aspens and firs, and a spectacular gorge dropping abruptly from sagebrush hills.

Rising at the Continental Divide deep within the San Juan Mountains of southern Colorado, the Rio Grande begins its journey as a quintessential mountain stream, tumbling through meadows riotous with wildflowers against a backdrop of bald peaks. Escaping from the mountains, the river flows for 70 miles across the tortilla-flat San Luis Valley. In this extensive basin, larger than the combined area of several New England states, the featureless meanders of the river are too warm for trout. Only after entering New Mexico and carving a sinuous gorge that divides the northern half of the state in two does the river again support coldwater species.

Exiting the broad valley between the Sangre de Cristo and San Juan ranges, the mountain character of the Rio Grande disappears twenty miles north of Santa

8

Fe where the muddy Rio Chama enters from the west. South of Santa Fe, flood control and irrigation dams alter the nature of the river and its riparian vegetation. Through the desert, the Rio Grande is not much more than a veneer of fluid adobe obscuring the sands of the shallow riverbed. During dry years the river simply vanishes into the dust. The bosque, impassable thickets of cottonwood, willows, and tamarisk, marks the edge of the channel. In the southern half of New Mexico, Elephant Butte and Caballo Reservoirs create warmwater fisheries before the river dives along the Texas-Mexico border, turns broadly to the east, and finally reaches the Gulf of Mexico.

Unlike waterways that meet conventional expectations, the Rio Grande has many atypical ways. The river flows more than half its way to the sea before it is joined by a major tributary, the Pecos River. The upper 400 miles of the unnavigable river spawned no major cities, the first being Albuquerque near the

◆

The black patina of basalt boulders was a favorite canvas for rock artists of the Anasazi culture. Among the thousands of petroglyphs found in the canyons of the Rio Grande, shields, snakes, and game animals are common. Curiously, pictures of fish are exceedingly rare. Photo by Craig Martin

Beginning around the thirteenth century, the Anasazi people built multi-storied villages along the tributaries of the Rio Grande. Their descendants still live in pueblos scattered along the river. Photo by S. Brooks Bedwell

◆

river's transition to a desert stream. While most rivers follow their own water-worn valleys, half of this river flows along the 30,000-foot deep Rio Grande Rift, formed by the massive tensional forces of plate tectonics. From Del Norte to El Paso, the river follows the rift, which is filled with sediments washed down from the surrounding mountains.

The Anasazi culture built multi-storied stone and adobe pueblos along the Rio Grande beginning in the thirteenth century. Evidence of their long use of the land can be found in thousands of petroglyphs pecked into the black basalt within the river's canyons. Spanish conquistadors in search of gold and souls to save arrived on the Rio Grande in 1540, long before the settlements along the Atlantic seaboard were established. The first European colony on the Rio Grande was founded in 1598 near the river's confluence with the Rio Chama.

In the early days of European settlement, the Rio Grande suffered from an identity crisis. Spanish explorers encountering the river at different locations failed to see it as a single stream and attached no less than twelve names to its waters. As the geography of New Mexico and Texas was gradually sorted out, the river became known as the Rio del Norte, the River of the North, and the Rio Bravo, Bold River. After the conquest of New Mexico in 1846, American map makers gave the river its current name, but in Mexico it is still called the Rio Bravo.

The long history of three peoples is still reflected in the cultural mix of southern Colorado and New Mexico. The unique charm of the art, architecture, and lifestyle of those that live along the river is a blend of Native American, Spanish-Mexican, and late-arriving Anglo-American values. The Spanish influence is strong, as the melodious names on a map will attest.

Although a desert river for most of its course, the Rio Grande is born deep in the San Juan Mountains of Colorado.

Photo by Craig Martin

The Rio Grande in Colorado

The San Juan Mountains of southwestern Colorado are among the most rugged ranges in the lower forty-eight. The crinkled peaks, jutting as much as 7,000 feet above the surrounding basins, are sharp-toothed enough to earn the nickname "the American Alps." The range was born about 30 million years ago and grew through a protracted series of explosive eruptions from dozens of volcanoes. Much later, only in the last million years, glaciers carved the lofty summits into the spires and knife-edged ridges that characterize the range today.

Fed by deep snowfields that collect below the turrets of stone, the Rio Grande has evolved a course that borders at least five volcanic calderas, huge collapse craters formed after swan-song eruptions. In carving out its niche, the river pushed back the Continental Divide far to the west in what looks like a closed loop in a perfectly-cast fly line.

In Colorado, the Rio Grande is surrounded by an extensive wilderness. Less than 500 people live within the over 650 square miles of the watershed above Creede. This quiet forest rimmed in 13,000-foot peaks is isolated, far removed from the nearest big cities of Denver and Albuquerque, each over 300 miles away.

The angler who loves to fish a variety of waters will find it all on the Rio Grande. You can fish the river for a week and enjoy a different type of angling experience, from small streams to wide flats, every day. Hike-in water is plentiful in canyons, and drive-up, cast-from-your-car water is here, too. The connected valleys below Creede are big water, perfect for floating. With almost perfect habitat, an abundant food base, and a remote location, the upper river is a consistent producer of large trout. Not all fishermen come away pleased with the Rio Grande, but skilled and patient anglers will quickly fall under the river's spell.

The high country surrounding the Colorado portion of the Rio Grande offers an escape from the heat of summer. Days are cool, rarely reaching much above 80°F. Nights are decidedly chilly and mid-weight fleece pants and jackets are welcome for evenings around the campfire. Thunderstorms are a near-daily occurrence in summer, and anglers should carry rain gear wherever they go. Crisp fall days quickly give way to cold nights with frost possible anytime after early September. In winter, the Rio Grande freezes over.

The upper miles of the Rio Grande flow through inaccessible canyons and idyllic meadows at the base of the Continental Divide. Photo by Craig Martin

Dozens of small tributaries drain from the Weminuche Wilderness. Few fly fishing experiences can compare with strapping on a backpack and spending the day chasing trout along the rocky stream banks. Photo by June Fabryka-Martin

Headwaters of the Rio Grande

The headwaters of the Rio Grande were one of the last regions in the lower forty-eight to be opened up to settlers. Only mountain men in search of beaver pelts and explorer John Fremont, who came in search of a railroad route through the mountains, passed through the region before it was closed to whites by the Treaty of 1868. This agreement pushed the Ute Indians out of the San Luis Valley and into the San Juans, promising them exclusive use of the mountains. Just three years later, gold was discovered near Telluride and miners poured into the closed land. In 1873, the Utes were relocated a second time, and the Rio Grande headwaters were opened for settlement.

Few took a chance on living in the harsh environment, but the upper Rio Grande became an important part of the hunt for gold in the San Juans. The shortest route from the railhead at distant Pueblo to the new gold camps at Telluride and Silverton was across the San Luis Valley and up the Rio Grande to Stony Pass. Although it was not much more than a pack trail,

the first road over the pass opened in 1871. Food, tools, and heavy equipment were hauled 250 miles from Pueblo to the mines. The road was widened to accommodate wagons in 1879, but three years later most traffic along the Rio Grande stopped when the narrow gauge railroad connecting Silverton with Durango was completed.

At 10,000 feet above the sea, most rivers are merely cascades of water tripping over rocks, but at that elevation the Rio Grande is a fledgling river. A half dozen miles below Stony Pass, the diminutive stream gathers water from Pole and Bear Creeks and plunges into a wild canyon with near-impossible access. Below Timber Hill, the valley opens into lovely Brewster Park before squeezing through another bottleneck of rock and alternating between canyon and flats down to Lost Creek.

Where the river has room to roam, it eases down the valley beneath ramparts of buff-colored lava interfingered with bright aspens and somber firs. It's high country that makes it a challenge to keep your mind on fishing. The river is 10 to 15 feet wide as it winds among willows and turtle-shell rocks. At the outside of slow turns, the flow deepens and trout line up, watching for insects.

On midsummer mornings, water temperatures hover in the upper forties and the trout are lethargic. Around 11 a.m., mayflies and yellow stoneflies start to come off the water and the browns, brookies, and cutthroats begin feeding. They are fussier than most high-country trout, but take with confidence imitations that suit their fancy. Size 12 to 18 parachute mayfly imitations in brown, tan, gray, and yellow are perfect for this rippling water, with a few small hopper patterns thrown in for good measure. You'll find beautiful brook trout up to 12 inches, and the potential for browns up to 14 inches.

Not only does the upper Rio Grande offer quality fly fishing amid grand scenery, but the river's headwater tributaries do as well. Creeks draining the glacial valleys surrounding the river hold brook, brown and cutthroat trout up to 14 inches. Small rods, bushy flies, and stalking techniques are required to take fish in the pocket water and meadows of the creeks. With excellent trails leading along most of the streams, they tempt you with the promise of solitary backpacking trips into remote country.

The only trout found by trappers, prospectors and freighters traveling along the headwaters was the native Rio Grande cutthroat. This exquisite, bronze-washed, black-spotted trout has not been seen in the main stem of the Rio Grande for over fifty years. Unable to compete effectively with introduced browns, rainbows, brookies and other subspecies of cutthroat, the natives retreated into small headwater streams. According to John Alves of the Colorado Division of Wildlife, fifty-six populations of Rio Grande cutthroats, both natural and re-transplanted into parts of their former range, are found in Colorado. Only a few populations are located in the headwaters area—most of the natives are in the tiny creeks draining from the north and east into the San Luis Valley. Rio Grande cutthroats have also been eliminated from the main river in New Mexico where a similar number of populations are found in the small streams of the Sangre de Cristo and Jemez Mountains.

The vast basin of the headwaters funnels into a tight canyon that is now the site of Rio Grande Reservoir. The impoundment is the only major reservoir on the river's upper 300 miles. Completed in 1914, the reservoir is designed to regulate irrigation water for the agricultural fields of the San Luis Valley. Except in the flats near the inlet, steep banks and limited access make the stillwater unsuitable for fly fishing.

Below the reservoir the Rio Grande weaves a braided course through several miles of interconnecting channels on a narrow plain. Two campgrounds, Thirty Mile and River Hill, provide a convenient base of operations for fishing or simply enjoying the high country. Reach the campgrounds and the surrounding headwaters by taking Highway 149 west of Creede to Forest Road 520. Even with the road and campgrounds so close, angling is surprisingly good in this stretch.

For every river I know, the canyon reaches are my favorite part. It's not the size of the fish or their metropolitan numbers that lure me into rocky defiles, but the opportunity for total adventure. Shut off from the world, it's just me, tall cliffs, tumbled boulders, intricate patterns of water, and wild trout. At every pocket I have the sense, however false I know it to be, that I'm the first person to cast a fly onto the swirling surface.

From bottom to top, the Rio Grande flows through six major canyons. Three vertical-walled desert canyons—Boquillas, San Marical, and Santa Elena—nip at each others heels as the river arcs through half a circle at Big Bend along the Texas-Mexico border. It's a thousand miles upstream to White Rock Canyon where the river slices through the Cerros del Rio volcanic field, followed by the long gorge through the Taos Plateau. In Colorado, only Box Canyon and the impossible cataracts of the headwaters throw the river and its fish into seclusion.

Box Canyon is gouged out of the tan lavas below River Hill. The forest canopy hides the world beyond the river like the walls of a cozy den. As the Rio Grande squeezes through the confining cliffs, the channel is twenty to thirty feet wide. Much of the river is pocket water where it leaps over bedrock ledges and skips through long, choppy riffles. In other places, water melts quietly around boulders tumbled from the cliffs. Some pools are so lovely that breaking the surface with a cast seems profane.

The dense forest that laps up to the river banks is trail-less, making the six miles of Box Canyon the wildest, most primitive stretch of the Rio Grande in Colorado. Access from above at River Hill or below at the mouth of the canyon is difficult at best. No formal trails lead to or follow the river, and reaching the water requires at least a half mile of bushwhacking through fir forest and willow thickets. Following the rugged stream is hard work. Many sheer walls of rock drop to the river, forcing steep detours or frequent crossings, which are impossible during runoff. A short box canyon near the middle of this stretch blocks the way upstream or downstream.

During high flows in early summer, when the canyon can be run by skilled kayakers, angling is nearly impossible. The river fills its banks and creeps under overhanging vegetation, giving little space to maneuver and almost no room to cast. It is best to wait until August or September to venture into Box Canyon, but getting around remains difficult and wading dangerous. The small boulders and bedrock on the bottom are slick, but there is no need to wade deep. For safety,

A heavy concentration of black spots in the caudal region and tail characterizes the Rio Grande cutthroat, the native trout of the southeastern Colorado and New Mexico. Now restricted to only a few headwaters, this cutthroat was found in the main river a century ago. Photo by Craig Martin

◆

stay along the edges. Wear lightweight hippers or plan to wade wet. Carrying a four-piece, eight-foot, four- to five-weight travel rod will make the hike into the river a bit easier.

Wild trout swim the waters of the canyon in surprising numbers. Most are browns, with some rainbows and a few cutthroats and cutbow hybrids thrown in the mix. The average size of the fish is 12 to 14 inches. In the wild water, these fish can give you a spirited fight that belies their modest size.

In the swift currents of the canyon, the trout hold in small pockets of slack water. To find them, you need to cover every likely spot. Cast to slack water along the banks or at the foot of cliffs. Submersed rocks often protect good fish. Look for trout in the circles of slack current in front of and behind rocks. A few seconds of drift with a high-floating dry fly is usually enough to bring a strike from a trout.

With fewer insects to eat than their downstream cousins, trout in Box Canyon are opportunistic feeders. Stoneflies dominate the insect populations in the canyon and golden stones can provide good angling when runoff subsides in July. Fishing with rough water attractors—Humpys, House and Lots, Irresistibles, Renegades, Elk Hair Caddis—will suffice in most situations, but daily mayfly hatches make it a good idea to bring a supply of Brown Wulffs and Parachute Adams, size 12 to 16.

The Creede Area

When the Rio Grande breaks free of the confines of Box Canyon, it takes a well-deserved rest from chaotic tumbling waters and for the next 15 miles meanders across a flat-bottomed plain. After corkscrewing through the idyllic Antelope Park, the river flows atop the bed of a long-vanished lake that once filled the collapse crater of a volcano. Exiting the plain at the dramatic walls of Wagon Wheel Gap, the river continues along a narrow valley to South Fork.

The town of Creede is tucked into the claustrophobic canyon of Willow Creek about two miles above the Rio Grande. Silver was discovered at the Holy Moses Mine in 1889 and prospectors poured into the gulch like floodwaters from the surrounding hills. Creede was a typical boom city, swelling to over 10,000 residents in three years. Also typical were widespread gambling, frequent gunfights, an extensive red-light district, and a variety of seedy characters. In its heyday, Creede counted Marshall Bat Masterson and Bob Ford, immortalized in song as the dirty coward that shot Jesse James in the back, among its inhabitants.

Like the river that flows nearby, the town of Creede is a throwback to a simpler time. Despite years of struggle against floods, disastrous fires, and declining precious metal prices, the town is going strong. Dwarfed by a backdrop of towering cliffs, Creede is a place that is far removed from the normal tourist fare. The Underground Mining Museum offers a realistic glimpse into the backbreaking work that went on in the early days of the town, and the Creede Museum tells the tales of some of the town's more colorful residents. A plethora of shops are located on Creede Avenue, as well as an outdoor supplies store and a fly shop.

In the early 1980s, the Rio Grande near Creede held small numbers of wild brown trout and not much more. Recognizing the fine potential of the river, the Colorado Division of Wildlife (CDOW) brought in a strain of rainbows from the Colorado River. The rainbows took readily to the habitat and, with catch-and-release status applied, they became self-sustaining. Unfortunately, irregular flow patterns and possibly whirling disease have taken their toll. CDOW continues to stock rainbows from hatcheries infected with whirling disease, but the effects on the Rio Grande, where the disease has been present for many years, is undetermined. For whatever reasons, the rainbow population is not as large as it was in the early 1990s. The rainbows that remain are hearty, strong, and smart, with a few fish reaching 18 inches or more.

Brown trout remain the heart of the Creede area fishery. Possession and slot limits on browns were instituted when the rainbows were introduced, and the brown population thrives. They average from 12 to 14 inches and larger fish are common.

Special regulations apply from the Rio Grande Fisherman Access Area to Marshall Park Campground and from Willow Creek to Goose Creek. Angling is

◆

Stimulators, attractor dry flies with bushy white wings, and parachute patterns are the imitations of choice for the Rio Grande in Colorado. In most circumstances, select a pattern that can be easily spotted in fast-moving water. Photo by Craig Martin

The railroad tracks that once carried tons of silver from the mines at Creede, Colorado now provide anglers access to the Rio Grande along Highway 149. Photo by Craig Martin

restricted to flies and lures only. The water is catch-and-release for all rainbows, and a two-fish bag and possession limit for brown trout is in effect. The browns must be 12 inches or shorter.

The forty-mile stretch from Antelope Park to South Fork is a confusing mix of public and private land. Wading anglers can find public access at the Rio Grande Fishermen Access Area about eight miles west of Creede along Highway 149 and at Marshall Park Campground about four miles downstream. Below Creede, another seven-mile stretch of public water is found near Palisade Campground and through the CDOW's Coller State Wildlife Area. Either Palisade or Marshall Park, popular but small Forest Service campgrounds, will serve well as a base for fishing the Creede area.

The Rio Grande gains a lot of volume between the mouth of Box Canyon and Creede. Through the volcanic valleys and cliffs, the river ranges from forty to sixty feet wide. Pocket water is still present, but it is not as dominant as it is in the headwater section. Broad riffles, shallow gravel bars, submerged boulders, and deep current seams characterize the river. Within the grassy ancient lake bed around Creede, undercut banks and overhanging willows and alders provide plentiful shelter for feeding fish. With so much

cover for trout, it takes a half day to thoroughly fish a quarter mile of stream.

The best way to cover the long expanse of water around Creede is to float the river. Floating allows angling the stretches of river where wading access is blocked by private land and permits you to fish long stretches of river in a single day. With so much private land along the banks, low bridges, a few barbed wire fences strung across the river, and limited put-ins and take-outs, it is best to float this stretch with a guide.

Timing is important here. The river can be floated only during the high flows associated with runoff. However, during early runoff, from May to mid-June, water temperatures are too cold for insect activity and angling is poor. Warming temperatures in mid-June stimulate insect activity, and thus trout feeding. Conditions for floating are usually ideal from mid- to late June through late July, depending on winter snowpack. By August, low flows make floating impossible.

From around Creede to Wagon Wheel Gap, the Rio Grande flows through a flat-bottomed bowl filled with a luxuriant growth of tall grasses. After the river squeezes through the Gap, it enters a compressed narrows with talus walls and big in-stream boulders. The rest of the way to South Fork is along a straight and narrow, forested valley. Floating this stretch of the

Colorado columbine, the state flower of Colorado. Photo by Craig Martin

river offers wild scenery, long vistas, and lots of rock dodging. Fish are plentiful, but are somewhat smaller on average than those found downstream.

The best water on this float is on the private ranches just below Creede. Browns and rainbows up to 16 inches are found through Wagon Wheel Gap. The average size of the fish in this stretch is larger than that in the public water around Palisade Campground and the Coller Wildlife Area. Half-day and full-day trips are offered by several of the guest ranches along the river, and by outfitters in Durango and Gunnison.

Although wading this stretch limits the amount of water you can cover, the fishing can be excellent. In this big water, chest waders are required. Wading is tricky in the swift current and the uneven bottom. Cobbles and boulders on the bottom make for tough footing, and frequent drop-offs into deeper water require the caution of all anglers. Casting is easy from gravel bars and from mid-stream, with brush rarely a problem.

Either floating or wading, a long rod will help with fly presentation on the intricate currents of the upper Rio Grande. In-stream rocks and churning flows make a drag-free float difficult. To achieve the best drift, limit the length of line you have on the water. Make short casts and lift most of the line off the water with the long rod. Keep only a few feet of line and the leader on the water. Slack-line casts are important. When casting across the currents, use the rod tip to create waves in the line, or use S, curve, and reach casts.

Search for trout behind and in front of boulders, and in deep runs and pockets. Surprisingly large trout can be plucked from deep channels within a few feet of the bank. Rainbows are often found at mid-stream in the pockets and along the bottom of runs; browns prefer the stream edges, particularly beneath overhanging vegetation.

Stonefly hatches bring some dry fly action to the Creede area around the time of runoff, in early to mid-June. Orange Stimulators and Sofa Pillows size 6 to 10 are all that is necessary to induce some strikes. When the hatch occurs during runoff, the water is generally clear enough to fish the hatch in the quiet pockets along the edges, either by wading or from a boat. Fishing a stonefly pattern with a twitch across the surface can often bring a fish out of hiding. When runoff slows, watch for little salmon flies (*Pteronarcella*) in late June and golden stones (*Hesperoperla*) running through early July. Orange or Yellow Stimulators sizes 8 to 12 will provide plenty of action from mid-morning to mid-afternoon.

Some mayfly hatches occur in late morning throughout the summer. Brown, red, and yellow-bodied naturals bring frequent rises for a couple of hours at midday. More hatches occur in the evening when mayflies are joined by thick clouds of caddisflies. The low-angle sun catches a glint from each insect wing and the air above the river sparkles. Trout actively feed until past dark, taking white-winged attractor patterns like the House and Lot or Royal Wulff, parachute mayfly imitations, and particularly caddis. Nothing is so effective as a simple Elk Hair Caddis, size 10 in the early season and dropping to size 16 later, skittered across the surface.

Nymphs are particularly effective in the deep water of the runs. Abundant stoneflies are found in the rocks along the bottom. Big nymphs fished very deep take the nicer rainbows and browns. You'll have to seek out the deepest water to find the big ones.

If you can't float the Rio Grande near Creede, an excellent way to fish the best water is to take up lodging at one of the fine guest ranches along the river. For modest accommodations with good fishing, many anglers turn to the historic Wason Ranch just southeast of Creede. The cozy streamside cabins are filled with anglers attracted to the quality trout habitat offered by the river's gentle curves as it crosses the ranch. Families looking for more luxurious surroundings can check out the 4UR Ranch at Wagon Wheel Gap. The ranch offers luxurious quarters, fine dining, tennis courts, horseback rides, and angling on both the main river and Goose Creek, a picturesque tributary with an excellent reputation for trout. For more information about these and other guest ranches in the area, contact the Creede-Mineral County Chamber of Commerce.

At Wagon Wheel Gap, the Rio Grande cuts through a wall of volcanic rock. Big boulders tumbled down from the walls create excellent pocket water in the canyon, where a long rod helps with getting a drag-free float. Photo by Craig Martin

Floating and the Gold Medal Water

When Rio Grande exits from the mountains at the logging town of South Fork, its character changes dramatically. The river flows on a broad, cottonwood-lined floodplain beneath rolling hills splotched with juniper and piñon pine. Heading due east for Del Norte and the San Luis Valley, the stream gradient decreases and the river broadens up to 100 feet. The currents are gentle as the river pushes through deep runs, over gravel bars, and down wide riffles. The Rio Grande becomes a true "big river," and its trout habitat continues to expand.

In recognition of the fine habitat, abundant food supply and versatile angling potential, the section of the Rio Grande between South Fork and Del Norte has been designated by the Colorado Division of Wildlife as Gold Medal Water. This classification identifies outstanding water with a potential for producing trophy trout and is applied sparingly to only a dozen stretches of stream throughout the state. From the upper boundary of the Gold Medal Water at the Highway 149

bridge to the Rio Grande Canal diversion structure, angling is limited to artificial flies or lures only. A two-fish, 16 inches or longer limit is in effect for browns, and all rainbow trout must be immediately returned to the water.

The Gold Medal Water assuredly deserves its lasting reputation as a quality brown trout fishery. The size and numbers of trout in this stretch of the Rio Grande are exceptional. Wild browns predominate, with thousands of fish in 12- to 14-inch class in every mile of river and many fish up to 18 inches. Wild rainbows are similar in size but less common, and a few cutbow hybrids up to 18 inches are also found here. The fish are well-fed, healthy, smart and strong—everything wild trout should be.

In the Gold Medal Water, the river flows entirely through private land. Access for wading anglers is limited to state lease lands that surround the bridges on County Roads 17 and 18. The north bank of the river is open from Granger Bridge on County Road 18 two miles upstream, and downstream to County Road 17. From Twin Mountain Bridge on County Road 17, easy

19

Below Creede, the Rio Grande meanders across a flat-bottomed valley filled with a luxuriant growth of grasses. Photo by Craig Martin

access is found on both banks of the river. Current lease information is posted at the access points and anglers should check the latest access information before fishing from any of the bridges.

In the lease areas, the stream banks vary from grassy to willow-lined. Wading is usually no problem, but always keep in mind that this is big water and remain watchful of sudden drop-offs to deep water. High flows during runoff creates dangerous conditions. Chest-high water along the banks makes it impossible to get far into the stream. Good-sized brown trout often lie just off the banks and under the roots of willows in pockets along the edges. It is a challenge to wade without spooking a bevy of trout. Slogging through forceful currents and fighting through brush can make for an exhausting day of angling.

After 1995's unusually prolonged runoff, I gave wading the Gold Medal Water a try when flows finally dropped in late July. It was a lazy morning and low clouds, the remains of the previous night's thunderstorms, hung on the mountains like Santa Claus'

beard. Around 10 a.m., at least six species of mayfly strafed the water and the trout responded by snatching them whenever they touched the surface. I cast my Brown Wulff to the risers and hooked up with nice browns at every turn. The trout rose freely to dry flies from the cover of the rocks on the bottom of choppy runs from one to two feet deep.

By lunch, I caught and released more than twenty nice browns, a fine day's worth of fishing. But the clouds seemed reluctant to leave, encouraging the mayflies to keep up their dances, and the trout continued to feed well into the afternoon. With the overcast, I could take fine fish from lies within a couple rods' length from where I stood. No doubt about it: The Rio Grande fishes best on cloudy summer days.

As water levels drop in August, wading gets easier but the trout head for deeper water and are less likely to rise to dry flies. Nymph fishing through the deep runs and current seams along gravel bars works best from morning through afternoon. Late evening hatches of mayflies and caddis bring a rise just before the sun hides behind the saw-toothed western skyline.

Because of the sheer amount of river and the predominance of private land, the best way to fish the Gold Medal Water is by floating with an experienced guide. A typical full-day, eighteen-mile trip extends from the Coller Wildlife Area to Twin Mountain Bridge. Such a float covers an incredible amount of water that sees few fishermen. Because of private land, it is not a float-wade trip and, except at the state leases, you must stay in the boat.

It is a curious float trip, one that is by no means a wilderness excursion. The route parallels highways and passes through South Fork where a hundred houses sit right on the bank. Along the way, you find yourself casting to pillows of water near patio decks, chatting about fishing conditions with home owners, or getting an earful of gospel music pushed out their windows. The lower half of the stretch has a more scenic quality, gliding by lush cottonwood bottoms and grasslands that reach back to pastel hills.

As with floating the upper stretch around Creede, timing on the Gold Medal Water is critical. Full-tilt runoff is a bit too wild to float, and cold water temperatures keep the fish inactive. As runoff subsides,

flows in the 700 to 1400 cfs range are perfect. With this much water it is difficult or impossible to wade the river, so floating is the only effective way to catch the trout as they feed on the prolific insect hatches of June and July.

Tom Knopick of Duranglers Flies and Supplies in Durango floats the river during the early summer window about a dozen times a year. "The river fishes well when it's coming down after runoff," Knopick says. "Warmer water temperatures get the bugs active. Another important factor is the high flows cover the gravel bars along the river banks, providing excellent cover for large browns in fairly shallow water."

A five- or six-weight rod at least 8½ feet long is needed to power flies from the boat into the banks. The fish are not tippet shy, so Knopick suggests a stout, 2X or 3X on a six- to eight-foot leader. A wide-brimmed hat, sunglasses, and plenty of sunscreen are necessary for a pleasant float.

At higher flows, most big brown trout hold near the bank. During the float, most casts head into the bank. Knopick constantly reminds his clients, "Look for subtle structure. Just off shore the water goes deep-

Brown trout are the heart of the Gold Medal Water between South Fork and Del Norte. Photo by Craig Martin

er. On the bottom there is often a line between light and dark substrate. When you see it, aim your casts there."

The banks are grassy, rocky, or overhung with willows and alders. Small pockets along the bank are likely to hold good fish. "Put your fly an inch from the bank in the little pockets," Knopick says. "Time your casts, wait for a window of opportunity to place the fly in the perfect place."

If you manage to get your fly into such a pocket, it usually gets slammed by a two-pound brown trout that will get your heart racing.

Hatches are prolific from mid-June to late July. Salmonflies, known locally as the Orange Asher, kick off the insect parade, beginning their run about the second week in June. As they taper off a couple weeks later, little salmonflies and golden stones take over. The last weeks of June also bring a terrific hatch of green drakes. A large variety of beautifully colored small mayflies hatch throughout the period. In the evening, a ton of caddis swarm over the water.

It all adds up to some great angling from late June to August. The hatches are thick for a couple hours either side of noon and trout rise freely and frequently to take the naturals. If you are on the water from 10 a.m. to 2 p.m., the action can be constant. You'll be surrounded by big browns slashing the surface in their enthusiasm to take bugs, a situation that is quite unnerving. Clouds can enhance the already heavy hatches, and prolong the rise through late afternoon.

Knopick recommends beginning the day with moderately-weighted black Woolly Buggers in sizes 6 to 10 cast to the banks. It usually doesn't take long for trout to get interested. If you float a mile of river without getting hits from a bushel of trout, it is indeed a slow day.

As insects appear around 10 a.m., Knopick sug-

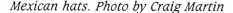

Mexican hats. Photo by Craig Martin

gests switching to Stimulators. Salmonflies are best matched with size 4 to 8 Orange Stimulators and a size 10 to 12 Royal Stimulator is an excellent pattern to imitate the smaller little salmonfly. The golden stonefly hatch can be fished with Yellow Stimulators in sizes 8 to 12.

Knopick starts fishing stonefly patterns with a dead drift, but if that simple technique fails to draw attention from trout, he tries twitching the pattern on the surface with a down or sideways shake of the rod. Brown trout often charge and grab stonefly patterns so hard that you'll almost jump out of the boat.

During the early summer blizzard of bugs, trout usually start looking for green drakes around 11 a.m. You can fish the hatch with a traditional size 12 Green Drake Dun, but Knopick suggests a different approach.

On a delightful trip down the river in the midst of the hatch, Knopick recommended fishing the hatch with the fluffy white wings and tail of a size 10 House and Lot, a pattern which bears as much resemblance to the real thing as a garlic cheese ball. I expressed my skepticism and Knopick suggested an experiment. Kevin Ott, my fishing partner and the better angler of the two of us, agreed to use a traditional, drab Green Drake Dun while I tried the House and Lot.

In the next fifteen minutes, ten heavy browns rushed from the rocks and gulped my white-winged pattern. In the back of the boat, Kevin went fishless. The point made, my partner frantically cut off the Green Drake and was all thumbs as he hastened to tie on the House and Lot.

Thoroughly amused, Knopick tried unsuccessfully to suppress his laugh. "It's old fly fishing wisdom that trout key in first on the size then the shape of the insect. Color seems to be the least important characteristic. Perhaps the white looks like shiny wings. Sometimes tempting them with a pattern a little bigger than the natural works wonders. You can't always figure the reason, but the H and L fools them time and time again."

As the hatches thin later in the day, there is often a sharp cutoff in feeding behavior. In the space of fifteen minutes, the trout suddenly shut down and you must resort to new tricks to garner attention from the trout. Knopick's favorite technique is to work a size 10 Dry Muddler aggressively across the surface. He suggests casting the Muddler tight against the bank and twitching it out across the feeding lanes. This technique is particularly effective along the grassy banks above Twin Mountain Bridge.

Near Del Norte, much of the Rio Grande's water is siphoned off to the fields of the San Luis Valley. Some fly fishing for pike is done in the slow-moving water of the valley, but trout anglers must take their search a hundred miles downstream to the lava flows of the Taos Plateau.

The rugged terrain of the seventy-mile long Rio Grande keeps many anglers away, but those who enjoy a total fly fishing adventure will find the Gorge a place of unique beauty. Photo by S. Brooks Bedwell

Overview of the Rio Grande Gorge

A half dozen miles above the Colorado-New Mexico border, Lobatos Bridge spans an insignificant dip that holds the Rio Grande. A few moment's float downstream, the river plunges suddenly from the monotony of the San Luis Valley into the volcanic rocks of the South Piñon Hills. It is an innocent beginning to what lies beyond—the seventy rugged miles of the Rio Grande Gorge.

My first day in the Rio Grande Gorge was a typical one. I carefully picked my way down a crack in a 600-foot cliff, losing my footing four times on ball-bearing rocks and sustaining multiple bruises and lacerations. I dodged two angry, buzzing rattlesnakes. Twice I slipped on glassy rocks along the river banks and fell in the water. I lost my concentration and missed three good fish when I paused to watch bald eagles glide thirty feet overhead, diving mergansers competing with me for trout, and a doe with a yearling feeding near a spring. Totally exhausted at the end of the day, I had to climb up the cliffs to my truck, losing two pounds of body weight in the process. For this extended effort I'd landed one trout. However, I was happy with the memory of that big brown that nearly bent my rod into a circle.

Beginners often find fishing the Rio Grande Gorge a frustrating experience. In truth, so do even the most experienced anglers. The Rio Grande is always interesting, always a challenge.

Van Beacham, owner of The Solitary Angler Guide Service, sums up the experience in a few words. "The Rio Grande Gorge is for anglers who enjoy trying to catch fish as much as they enjoy catching them."

Beacham has guided anglers on the Rio Grande for over twenty years and knows the fly fishing on the river as well as anyone. It's somehow fitting: Van's great-grandfather, William Beacham, helped introduce fly fishing to New Mexico when he moved from Boston in 1908 and began selling flies and gear from his hardware store in Santa Fe.

Fifty years ago, some of the best brown trout fishing in the west was found between the walls of the Rio Grande Gorge. Articles in several national outdoor magazines helped establish the river's reputation as one of the premier trout fisheries in the west. Noted angling author and Santa Fe resident Jack Samson recalls catching several eight- or nine-pound brown trout on spinning tackle near the confluence with the Red River in the late 1940s.

Conditions on the river changed in the 1960s when water quality and quantity were affected by upstream agriculture and mining on tributary streams. These factors served to exacerbate an extended period of low precipitation that led to low flows and high siltation in the river. For more than twenty years, angling experienced a steady decline.

Happily, the last several years have brought a reversal of this trend. Van Beacham says the Rio Grande is fishing better than he's ever seen it.

"The river is constantly improving," Beacham says with a northern New Mexico twang that belies his gentile English background.

Beacham believes it's part of a long-term trend. "The last ten or twelve years have been wet ones with strong runoff," he says with obvious excitement. "It's washed much of the river gravel clean, bringing back healthy populations of insects that can support more and larger trout. We've had more water coming down from Colorado and the local mines have shut down, but those factors haven't helped the river so much as the natural flushing flow we've experienced recently."

River watchers have seen a dramatic increase in the number of insects hatching on the river, particularly mayflies and caddisflies. Beacham claims the increasing food supply has helped take the average, skinny 12-inch brown trout formerly caught in the Gorge and turned it into a fat, 14-inch fish.

"Now they have some girth and spunk," Beacham says, wrapping his hands around a stout imaginary brown. Most of the fish in the Gorge are wild trout and Beacham estimates that over 80 percent of the fish he sees are unmarked, a sign of never having been caught.

Angling in the Gorge is highly technical fly fishing,

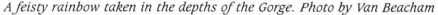

A feisty rainbow taken in the depths of the Gorge. Photo by Van Beacham

Flowing from two hundred to one thousand feet below the rim, fishing the Rio Grande in the Gorge requires a heart-pounding hike. Developed trails in the Wild and Scenic River section offer relatively easy access to the river. Photo by S. Brooks Bedwell

The plentiful shady pools on the Red River are formed by jumbles of basalt boulders. The Red provides important spawning areas for Rio Grande trout.

although it's not about delicate presentations and matching the hatch. It's a return to the days of wild, free-flowing rivers where you must seek out each fish and get your fly in the right spot to have a chance at catching them. It takes heavy rods, weighted flies, and the patience to make a hundred casts before you hook up with a fish.

Even without the trout, a trip into the Gorge is worthwhile. Any hike into this untamed landscape is a total adventure, a chance to explore a true wilderness. The Gorge is a sanctuary for wildlife and bald and golden eagles, geese, mergansers, herons, elk, deer and antelope are part of the Gorge experience. Every day spent between the walls of lava is unforgettable.

Adding to the challenge is the structure of the Gorge. Starting about 10 million years ago, the Rio Grande Rift near Taos began filling with lava erupted from more than ten shield volcanoes. On its way south, the river was forced to cut through the lava, carving out the Gorge in the last three million years. As a result, the river flows 200 to 900 feet below the surface of the plateau.

◆

Cliff dwellings at Bandelier National Monument. Photo by S. Brooks Bedwell

Like a ribbon of gold inside a castle, the Rio Grande is protected by solid, unscalable walls of stone. Only two river-level road access points are found in the seventy miles of gorge from Lobatos to Pilar. That creates a lot of hike-in-only water. A maze of axle-twisting dirt roads and a few paved ones lead to the rim of the Gorge where over a dozen trails and primitive routes make the drop from rim to river. Each trail is guaranteed to stress a knee on the way down and exhaust you on the climb back out.

The river itself is powerful and turbulent, dropping an average of thirty feet per mile through the Gorge. Wading such currents is tough and often dangerous. Deep sand or gravel make up short segments of the bank, but more often the river's edge is cluttered with rocks. Moving up or down stream requires a good deal of boulder-hopping on water-washed basalt. Every rock surface, whether wet or dry, is slick. Casting from such rocks is awkward at best, but the banks frequently offer little choice. Boulders as long as a ten-wheeler frequently block the route along the banks, forcing a long detour or disappointing retreat to continue.

The Rio Grande Gorge is simply a rough, rugged, potentially hazardous place to fish. Locals have an oft-quoted expression: A successful day in the Gorge is when you come out alive. Believe it!

Obviously, careful planning is required to make a safe trip into the Gorge. It's a full-day adventure, so stuff a large volume backpack with reel, vest, lunch, sunblock, and a half gallon of water. Dress in layers so you can adjust to the wide range of temperatures experienced along the river in the course of the day. Wading is generally unnecessary in the Gorge, so leave your waders behind or throw them in your pack and carry them to the river. For ankle support, wear a pair of sturdy hiking boots on the hike from the rim and while walking along the rocky banks. Carry an eight-and-a-half to nine-foot, five- or six-weight rod in its protective case on your way down. At the end of the day, allow plenty of time to work your way back to your car—it's miserable to pick your route up the canyon walls in failing light.

The 6,000-foot elevation of the Gorge creates unusual weather conditions for a trout stream. Winter temperatures in the Gorge range from surprisingly mild to frigid, and sunny days are best for any trip. Be watchful for snowstorms that can quickly rumble in from the west. Spring winds blow constantly and create frustrating casting conditions. In summer, when intense sunshine and reflection from the canyon walls can produce temperatures approaching the century mark, early morning and evening fishing are most comfortable. Fall conditions are often ideal, but blowing snow riding a cold front is possible anytime after late September.

Water conditions throughout the Gorge vary with the seasons. In winter, the river is low and clear and often fishes well except during the coldest weather. Spring runoff usually begins in mid-April and turns the river into a churning mudbath that is dangerous and unfishable. The river is fickle in summer, varying from murky to muddy as powerful thunderstorms in the surrounding country wash mud into the tributary streams and thence into the river. Anglers look to fall with its bright, clear days as the prime season to fish the Gorge.

The entire Gorge from the Colorado state line to Taos Junction Bridge in the Orilla Verde Recreation Area has been designated as Special Trout Water by the New Mexico Department of Game and Fish. No tackle restrictions are in effect, but the limit is four trout of any size per day or in possession.

Taos is the standard base of operations for a trip to the Rio Grande Gorge. The eccentric old town is a microcosm of New Mexico, a curious mix of Spanish, Native American, and Anglo cultures. Visitors can tour the town's plaza and historic churches, see famed scout Kit Carson's house, and learn about life in early Spanish New Mexico at the Martinez Hacienda. Nearby Taos Pueblo offers a glimpse of a village that has been inhabited by Native Americans for 900 years. The town's rich artistic heritage is celebrated in dozens of art galleries and several fine museums, such as the Millicent Rogers Museum. A fly shop is located on the main street through town.

If your outdoor interests extend beyond angling, the domes of the Sangre de Cristo Mountains, rising abruptly east of town, will beckon. The mountains offer endless opportunity for hiking in Carson National Forest and the Latir, Wheeler Peak, and Pecos Wilderness Areas. Hundreds of miles of mountain bike trails provide some of the state's finest single track riding. Along the river itself, numerous outfitters run float trips through the Taos Box.

Further south but still within an hour's drive of the lower Gorge lies Santa Fe, one of the country's oldest and most unique cities. The early history of Spanish New Mexico is well-told at the Palace of the Governors and other historic buildings near the plaza. Around town, museums are dedicated to fine, Indian, and folk art. Shops and galleries offer the finest works by southwestern artists. Nearby, the ruined villages at Bandelier National Monument offer the chance to walk amid the homes of the vanished Anasazi. A fly shop and guide services are located in the city.

Ute Mountain Run

As it skirts around the inverted bowl of Ute Mountain, the Rio Grande does its warmups, barely attacking the surface of the Taos Plateau. The upper-most stretch of the Gorge—from Lobatos Bridge thirty miles south to Lees Crossing—deepens to only 200 feet. As you approach on the plateau, the canyon is hidden from view until you reach the very edge. The angling matches the Gorge itself—rugged, wild, demanding. Those who make the arduous journey into the Ute Mountain Run must work hard to catch a few fish.

The Ute Mountain Run is my favorite stretch of the Gorge. Not many people venture into this rugged wilderness of rock and river. Once you take three steps from the rim, you find yourself immersed in the Gorge and cut off from the rest of the world. The low, tight canyon walls and the gentle nature of the river give this stretch an intimate feel and it is easy to lose yourself in the grandeur of the canyon. Small details of the Gorge stand out: Brilliant green leaves of watercress growing in hundreds of springs along the foot of the cliffs; red vines draped over boulders like waterfalls of flame; and pillowy black walls of lava that plunge into the river.

A large proportion of the water that flows beneath Lobatos Bridge is irrigation return water from the hay and potato fields of the San Luis Valley. In the Ute Mountain Run, thousands of natural springs feed cooling water into the river, just barely returning the Rio Grande to coldwater fishery status. Summer water temperatures in the upper Gorge are too high for consistent angling and the Ute Mountain Run is almost exclusively a fall fishery.

The character of the Rio Grande in the Ute Mountain Run is strikingly different from that in other sections of the Gorge. Low stream gradients create long flats, wide turns, and short riffles. Holding water for trout is scattered, and trout are few and far between.

As if to compensate for the lack of habitat, the river is incredibly rich. Any trout that finds a protective lie has a constant supply of food coming by on the currents. Few insects are found here, but trout have an abundant supply of minnows, suckers and other forage fish, supplemented by some jumbo crayfish. As a result, the fish in the upper Gorge grow fast. The few rainbows and cutthroat hybrids found here average 14 inches. Browns can grow to monstrous proportions: five-pound fish are not unusual.

A rutted dirt road leaves the highway ten miles north of Questa and leads west to the lower half of the Ute Mountain Run. As you bounce along the road across waves of sagebrush-covered hills, it is difficult to imagine that a trout lives within fifty miles. A high-clearance vehicle will get you to the double tracks above the river. Lees Trail at the bottom of the run is the only maintained trail into the section, but there are numerous primitive routes on which you can work your way down the cliffs.

The lack of prolific insect hatches in the run means these trout almost never feed on the surface. Dry fly fishermen have but a few windows in which to operate. In summer, evening hatches of caddisflies can create sporadic surface activity. Casting to rising fish is a successful technique, drifting Elk Hair or Goddard Caddis patterns sizes 12 to 16 over the feeding stations. Using wet flies is often more productive. Fish wet flies dead drift in the current, or with a slow cross-current swing. Fall brings reliable hatches of blue-winged olives from late September to late November.

Most trout hold and feed near the bottom throughout the year. The trick to hooking up with one of the big browns is putting big flies where the fish are. It takes heavily-weighted nymphs or streamers to reach the fish, and often you must add some weight to the leader six inches to a foot above the fly. Begin with a general attractor like a bead-headed Gold Ribbed Hare's Ear or Prince Nymph, size 6 to 10. Caddis lar-

◆

Both pocket water and deep runs are found in Box Canyon. Although cliffs and fir forest squeeze against the river and make access difficult, the wild trout in the canyon make the effort worthwhile. Photo by Jessica Martin

vae, particularly green *Rhyacophilia* "worms," are also important to trout.

If nymphs fail to find any fish, go to streamers. Brown and Yellow Bucktails, Little Brown Trout streamers, and brown Marabou Muddlers often produce well. Don't be afraid to use patterns up to size 4. Try a down-and-across, slow swing to pull the fly through every deep hole you can find. Large crayfish are found in the slowest water, and crayfish imitations fished with a jerky, swimming motion are often an irresistible temptation to large browns.

Because holding water is scant, you want to make certain you are in the best possible position before each cast. You can't afford to waste a potential lie with poor presentation. You can ignore most shallow water, but don't overlook the rocky edges of deep flats where good fish often lie protected by the rocks. In the deep runs, cast well upstream of your target area to give the fly plenty of time to sink. Keep the line tight as your pattern bounces along the bottom.

From Lobatos Bridge to Lees Trail is by far the easiest stretch of the Gorge to float. Flows are frequently too low for watercraft until upstream irrigation stops in mid-September. It's an unpredictable trip, and once you start you are committed to the river for at least three days. Access is limited to the put-in at Lobatos and the take-out at Lees Trail, where packing your gear out of the Gorge is necessary. For more information on floating this section, contact the Taos Area Office of the Bureau of Land Management at (505)758-8851.

Wild and Scenic River Section

Below the placid waters of the Ute Mountain Run, the Gorge quickly doubles its depth and the river thunders through a tumultuous stretch of whitewater. As if the river needed some breathing room after its journey through the confines of the Gorge above, the canyon walls spread apart. The Gorge is at its grandest above the confluence with the Red River as towering cliffs, tall pines, and the tumbling river combine to paint an expansive mural.

In 1968, Congress created the Rio Grande Wild and Scenic River, the first of its kind. West of the village of Cerro on Highway 378, the Wild and Scenic River Recreation Area provides relatively easy access into the Gorge—if you consider a thousand-foot drop to the river on well-graded trails a piece of cake, which it is compared to most nearby rim-to-river routes. A visitor center and four campgrounds are located on the rim, as well as trailheads to the river. The Big Arsenic, Little Arsenic, and La Junta trails drop to the river in a little over a mile, and another trail connects the three at the

Big browns in the Ute Mountain Run often feed on crayfish. Actively fishing a crayfish imitation along the bottom is one of the best ways to find the browns. Photo by Craig Martin

◆

bottom. Campsites with shelters sit on the bench just above the river. Easy access brings lots of anglers to this stretch, but the size of the river allows them to spread out and the Gorge never feels crowded.

Although the canyon is wide in this stretch, the Rio Grande itself is confined in a narrow inner gorge. The flow from natural springs, as well as shade from the towering walls, drop the water temperature. The river is one long cascade. For miles the banks are stacked with great hunks of basalt fallen from the cliffs above. Herds of rocks are found in the currents, creating some of the best pocket water found in the West. Breaking up the pocket water are plenty of plunge pools and a few riffles. Long, deep runs form below many of the monster in-stream boulders. This section of the river is floated by only the most experienced boaters.

The worn-smooth basalt that lines the river makes for slow movement along the banks. In the river, deep holes are everywhere and wading is treacherous. In a single step, the water can go from one to ten feet deep. Fast currents add to the hazards. It is best to avoid wading and to cast from the bank.

The abundance of holding water makes for a large number of fish. Most of the trout are rainbows and browns, but some cutbow hybrids are also found here. Many fish are in the 14-inch class, and it is not unusual to find a grandfather brown up to five pounds.

With so much water and so many potential lies, it's difficult to figure out where to put a fly. Master angler Taylor Streit has guided on the Rio Grande for twenty years and believes that developing a sense of the right water is more important to success on the Rio Grande than fly pattern or presentation.

"It takes a long time to get to know this river," Streit says with a knowing shake of this head. "There's lots of dead water, lots of places teeming with fish, concentrating where the food does. You have to learn to find the right water. Just the right current speed, the right choppiness, the proper depth."

Streit has a piece of important advice for newcomers to the Rio Grande. "Flash floods pump tons of silt into the river. It accumulates in the slower water, covering the gravel and insect beds. In all the river, fish seek the faster water, where the food is. You'll find lots of trout in slicks, quick little runs, and the heads of pools. One of the keys to this river is to ignore the silty stretches and concentrate your efforts where the gravels are washed clean. Study the bottom carefully before making your first cast."

Nymph and streamer fishing are popular and productive in the pocket water of the Wild and Scenic River section. Streit has a simple explanation of their success.

"Fish consistently take nymphs because they are used to looking down for their food," Streit says. He believes that bottom feeding accounts for an overwhelming proportion of the trouts' diet.

All kinds of nymphs can be effective in the Gorge, but as a general rule large patterns—size 4 to 10—attract the most attention. Fishing nymphs in the Wild and Scenic River section requires the patience of a saint, searching for trout around every rock in the river, as well as through the deepest part of the long runs below plunge pools. Use a small strike indicator for all nymph fishing on the Rio Grande. Trout lying

◆

Sunset on the rim of the Rio Grande Gorge in the Wild and Scenic River section. Photo by S. Brooks Bedwell

The Gorge produces big brown trout. Photo by Van Beacham

deep rarely grab a fly and run, but will quietly sip an imitation. An indicator will help you detect subtle takes. When your indicator deviates from a normal drift, pull back gently on the rod to set the hook.

The local favorite nymph is the Double Hackle Peacock, an elongated variation of the Renegade. Shimmering peacock has an almost magical ability to attract Rio Grande trout. Fish the Peacock heavily weighted, dragging it along the bottom. Cast well upstream from a suspected lie to give the fly plenty of time to sink. If you aren't feeling the nymph bounce along or occasionally snag the bottom, you probably aren't using enough weight. Add some weight to the leader and try again until you are certain your imitation is down as far as it will go.

Taylor Streit offers his Poundmeister nymph as an alternative to the standard peacock pattern. A variation of the traditional Muskrat, Streit developed the Poundmeister specifically for bottom-feeding Rio Grande trout.

"When the trout hit but won't take the Peacock nymph, I switch to the Poundmeister," Streit says. "For whatever reason, I get fewer hits but surer takes with it."

In big water, big patterns are often the most effective way to cover lots of water, and streamers provide this wide-area coverage. Brown and Yellow Bucktails are successful here, probably because of their resemblance to brown trout fry. Black Woolly Buggers also receive a fair amount of attention from trout. In fall, browns constantly dart out from the cover of rocks to charge at streamers. Streamers can be fished dead drift along the bottom, or on the swing in front of rocks and through pockets.

A few hatches bring trout to the top during summer. In early to mid-July, a nice little hatch of pale mornings duns occurs on most days, particularly on cloudy mornings. Late July and August brings a more reliable hatch of size 10 ginger mayflies. Ginger-bodied imitations with elk hair wings, tied either standard or parachute-style, are best for matching this insect. Use the usual Rio Grande *modus operandi* for dry flies: cast to rising fish. Typically fishing is not very productive in the afternoon when it is better to fish one of the tributary streams until evening.

The most consistent hatch in the Wild and Scenic River section is the fall occurrence of blue-winged olives. The delicate insects are on the surface from 11 a.m. to 3 p.m. Trout lazily feed on them in moderate currents, but not in the more turbulent pocket water. The fish line up along bubble lines where the insects are concentrated. Soft casts of Parachute Blue-winged Olive patterns size 16 to 20 will take rising fish. You'll find you may take a half dozen fish from a fifty-foot run, then not find another in the next quarter mile.

Hundreds of natural springs in the area help moderate winter water temperatures and the Wild and Scenic River Area can be fished year-round, except during runoff. Mild days in winter are particularly inviting. Despite wildly fluctuating air temperatures, the water stays between 38° and 40°F. Midges and mayfly nymphs are most effective during the cold months. A note of caution: When the trails into the Wild and Scenic River are snow covered, they are dangerous. Because it's too easy to break a leg, give the snow a few days to melt away before venturing on the trails.

La Junta Run

Although the Rio Grande is a free-flowing, wild river, it is not immune to the effects of man. The La Junta Run and the Red River, a tributary that joins the Rio Grande at the head of the run, are the center of a long-term controversy centered on molybdenum mining on the steep slopes of the Red River canyon.

In the late 1970s and early 1980s, dozens of pipeline breaks at the Molycorp Questa mine resulted in the spillage of raw tailings into the Red River. The metal-laden sediments flowed into the Rio Grande, covering the river bottom with toxic mud. Insect populations in the La Junta Run were decimated, and with them, the trout.

A federal lawsuit required the mine to upgrade its delivery system, but the tailings pipeline connecting the mine with ponds near Questa remains along the banks of the Red River, inviting disaster. Molycorp contends that since the spills they have not contributed any heavy metal contamination to the river. Amigos Bravos, a river watchdog group based in Taos, claims that seepage from over 300 million tons of waste rock continues to reach the Red River, and thus the Rio Grande, through groundwater movement. Molycorp counters that the tailings pits are lined with a barrier that prohibits the movement of acidic leachate into the environment and that any contamination in the rivers is due to natural leaching from metal-rich rock.

In 1992, molybdenum prices dropped below $2 per pound and the Questa mine shut down operations. Following this and several years of above average precipitation, anglers noticed a steady improvement in the fishing in the Red River and the La Junta Run. Caddis populations increased, along with a trend toward larger, stronger trout. However, in early 1996 molybdenum prices climbed to a level where the Questa mine could again be profitable and Molycorp resumed mining operations along the Red River in July of that year.

As Taylor Streit says, "On a scale of one to ten, the Rio Grande fluctuates between a six and a nine, depending on the price of molybdenum."

Anglers anxiously wait to see if renewed mining will effect the rivers and their trout. As a biological assessment of the river has never been done, any changes in siltation or the insect and trout populations will be difficult to document. It's a shoddy way to treat the nation's first Wild and Scenic River.

The river structure in the La Junta Run is better than in any other stretch of the Gorge. The Run is well-known for its insect-producing riffles. Long stretches of the river flow over a bottom of smooth cobbles, which provide the breeding ground and protection for

◆

Seven steep trails take hikers from rim to river in the Wild and Scenic River section. Photo by S. Brooks Bedwell

Winter nymphing on the Red River. Photo by Van Beacham

♦

excellent populations of stoneflies and caddis. The dominance of riffles is broken by glassy flats pierced by rounded boulders, and deep runs that push hard against the banks. Occasional sharp drops in the river bed create slicks that empty into swirling eddies and short pools. In short, the La Junta Run allows you to pick your favorite type of water.

With abundant food and protection, trout are plentiful. Stocked rainbows work upstream from the barrels spilled at the John Dunn Bridge and quite a few of these fish survive to reproduce in the river, giving the area a nice population of wild rainbows. Brown trout are common, but are not known to reach the proportions of the fish in the river upstream. Most fish are in the 10- to 14-inch class.

River systems usually display a tree-like pattern, but the Rio Grande in New Mexico lacks a thick tangle of tributaries. A few creeks drain from the Sangre de Cristo Mountains, scouring out their own miniature gorges to reach the river. Most notable of these sparse tributaries is the Red River, whose confluence with the Rio Grande defines the head of the La Junta Run.

Although less than fifteen feet across, the Red River is a fine trout stream in its own right. Bouldery pockets, picturesque plunge pools and overhanging willows make the Red a challenge to fly fish. Its tumbling waters can hold surprisingly large fish that work their way up from the main river. When the Rio Grande is muddy, warm, or just not fishing well, plopping nymphs into the Red or drifting Blue-winged Olives on its surface can save the day.

Despite the river's reputation as a subsurface stream, in the past several years dry flies have become more effective on the Rio Grande. With improving conditions and increasing numbers of insects, even the larger fish are taking adult insects. More so now than any time in the last few decades, matching the hatch can be an important technique, particularly in the insect-rich riffles of the La Junta Run.

Two important caddisfly hatches occur in spring. The first caddis is a small, black-bodied bug, the second a brown-winged *Brachycentrus.* Both hatches are prolific. When it occurs, rocks, grasses, trees and anything taller than a grasshopper are dressed in fluffy

34

The Red River just above its confluence with the Rio Grande and the start of the La Junta Run. The water quality in the Red River greatly affects the quality of angling in the La Junta section. Photo by S. Brooks Bedwell

In spring, the long riffles of the La Junta Run produce heavy hatches of caddisflies, the most consistent hatch on the river. Photo by Van Beacham

◆

wings. In clumsy flight, the insects will fly into your ears and eyes, and if you open your mouth a bit too wide, you might get to imitate a trout and taste a stray caddis.

The first hatch begins around Embudo in early April, moving up river about a mile a day. The second hatch follows one to two weeks behind. The peak of caddis fishing on the La Junta Run comes the second or third week in April, but the insects continue a thin showing until mid-May.

As is often the case with spring hatches on Western rivers, these fine hatches usually coincide with runoff. While it is possible to catch trout blindly slashing at insects in muddy, turbulent water, fishing the hatch is more fun (and less hazardous) when runoff is delayed by cool spring temperatures or below normal snowpack.

Pre-runoff caddis angling is superb and offers the easiest fly fishing you'll ever see in the Rio Grande Gorge. In a river where most of the time the fish are difficult to spot, the caddisflies bring trout to the surface, feeding with abandon. By 11 a.m. the trout eagerly seek caddis drifting on the water. The fish concentrate on insects that collect along current seams. If you can spot a seam of caddis floating on the surface, watch for rising trout taking them. You won't be successful searching for trout: Cast only to rising fish. At this time, trout rarely feed in mid-stream or in swift water, but work near tall rocks along the banks and in idle currents just offshore. It's not unusual to find a

◆

Cranefly larva and imitation. Photo by Craig Martin

Rugged lava cliffs dominate the Taos Box below John Dunn Bridge. Photo by Craig Martin

half dozen good fish feeding along a seam between an eddy and the main current.

Most anglers are content to use a standard Elk Hair Caddis to fish both the hatches, but a tan-bodied version is often more effective. Start the day with a size 14 imitation, changing to a size 16 as the day wears on, or if the larger pattern is constantly refused. Any caddis pattern will garner more attention if fished actively. Skittering your pattern across the surface in a series of short jumps can bring slashing rises from good-sized trout.

The riffles of the La Junta Run also produce nice hatches of blue-winged olives from late September through November and into December. Trout rise to the naturals during the warmest part of the day, from noon to 2 p.m. The delicate insects are concentrated along bubble lines, which is where you find rising trout. Watch the bubble lines carefully and cast to risers.

Other less important hatches do occur. At the end of runoff, a light hatch of size 14 brown stoneflies (*Capnia*) comes off, accompanied by a very thin hatch of salmonflies. A nice little hatch of size 8 golden stoneflies follows. Size 10 ginger duns come off in August, and the hatch stimulates lots of feeding activity in the evening. Fishing large cream cranefly larvae along the bottom is another effective fish getter.

In this reach of the Gorge, the outpouring of lava from the surrounding volcanoes was highly variable and the canyon walls range from 300 to 800 feet high. The Cebolla Mesa Trail on Forest Road 9, fifteen miles north of Taos, drops 900 feet to the top of the run. The bottom of the run is at the John Dunn Bridge west of Arroyo Hondo, the only river-level access in the upper Gorge. In between, five miles of rutted double track north of the John Dunn Bridge lead to an old mining trail near Cedar Springs that drops from the west rim to the river.

At the bottom of the La Junta Run lies a bridge that has long been one of the few crossings of the Rio Grande in northern New Mexico. The first bridge built at the site was purchased around 1900 by John Dunn of Taos. He bought the bridge with $2300 he earned the old-fashioned way—gambling. The bridge business was quite a gamble, too. Shortly after he bought the structure, spring runoff washed out the bridge

The volcanoes of the Taos Plateau oozed more than 50 cubic miles of lava. Through the rugged Taos Box, the Rio Grande flows at the bottom of a deeply incised gorge sliced into the level plain formed by lava flows. Photo by S. Brooks Bedwell

◆

forcing Dunn to take another chance and rebuild it. The enterprising toll keeper started a stage line to connect Taos with the nearest railroad station at Sevilleta, established a hotel and restaurant at the mouth of the Rio Hondo, and later ran a taxi service over the hair-raising road across the Gorge. Dunn's original bridge with stone and log pilings is gone, replaced by a more modern steel structure.

The La Junta Run provides the most consistent float fishing in the Gorge. The Run is a moderately difficult float with only a few Class IV rapids. Trips begin with a hike down the Cebolla Mesa Trail and end at the John Dunn Bridge, with a leisurely two days of floating and wading in between. Trips are offered by commercial outfitters in Taos.

Taos Box

After flowing placidly beneath John Dunn Bridge, the river somersaults into the wildest section of the Rio Grande Gorge, the Taos Box. The slash through the lava narrows and deepens to as much as 1,000 feet. To get to the water in this stretch you have to be part crazy old prospector and part crazy old prospector's mule.

To get a feel for the rough-edged nature of the ter-

rain in the Taos Box, take a drive over the Rio Grande Gorge Bridge on Highway 64 just west of Taos. The bridge spans the Gorge at one of its narrowest points. When you reach the edge of the Gorge after miles of driving over rolling sagebrush plain, the bottom of the world seems to drop out from under your car. Even when you know what to expect, the effect is dizzying.

In the Taos Box, the river alternates between turbulent and calm, but foaming water prevails. Class V rapids line up like a string of pearls, and the river receives heavy use by experienced whitewater rafters. For the angler, the river consists of pools, rapids, riffles and pocket water. The back-breaking trails that drop through the walls will take your breath away. They are slick, stair-step affairs that can lead you to the brink of disaster. At river level, the constricting walls leave little room to maneuver along the banks. You often find that the knee-pounding work required to get to the water has left you with only a couple hundred yards of stream to work with. The Taos Box is not user-friendly.

Paradoxically, at the head of the Taos Box lies the easiest access to the river within the Gorge other than the John Dunn Bridge. In the 1890s, a couple of ambitious Taos merchants widened an ancient trail into a white-knuckle wagon road, built a bridge across the river, and blasted a route up the other side, thus connecting Taos by stagecoach to the nearest railroad station at Tres Piedras. Near the river, stone walls of a bath house built by Arthur Manby, a conniving Taos resident with a predilection for unworkable get-rich-quick schemes, enclose a hot spring.

The old stagecoach road to the hot springs drops a mere 400 feet from rim to river on gentle grades. It plants you smack in the middle of wild country. From the hot springs you can work upstream a mile to the John Dunn Bridge, or downstream where anglers rarely venture.

The hot springs area shares many characteristics with the La Junta Run. A few rainbows come down from the bridge, but most of the trout in the Taos Box are wild browns. The browns usually stay close to the bottom, feeding on stonefly nymphs, caddis larvae, and forage fish. It's chuck-and-duck fishing, throwing out heavily-weighted nymphs to rocks, seams, and pockets. The spring caddis hatch will bring trout to the surface, and winter midge fishing around the hot springs can be excellent. As the gorge narrows below the springs, the canyon becomes treacherous.

Orilla Verde Recreation Area Near Pilar

Another strange twist to this river of mystery is that excellent dry-fly fishing can be had in the dead of winter. When the Sangre de Cristos have donned their white winter caps, swarms of insects hover over the icy water like a fine mist. Instead of vegetating the afternoon away in front of a dull football game on television, knowing anglers head to the Rio Grande for the snowfly hatch.

Snowflies are a prolific midge hatch and can be found on the river every day from early December through February. The tiny insects—no larger than size 24—skim the water during the afternoon. It is not unusual to find the surface of a pool almost covered with midges.

Although the snowfly hatch occurs through almost

Fishing big streamers along rocky banks is an effective way to take trout throughout the Gorge, particularly in the fall. Photo by June Fabryka-Martin

Hedgehog cactus flowers. Photo by Craig Martin

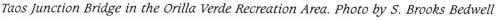

push apart, giving the river a bit of elbow room. The river calms and widens. Wading is easy on gravel bars and along the banks, although deep holes can still swallow an unwary angler. Little pocket water is found in this stretch, and most of the river is comprised of deep runs, riffles and featureless flats.

Effective techniques for fishing the snowfly hatch go against most conventional angling wisdom. My first half dozen trips to Pilar for winter trout gave me nothing but chilled bones, frozen fingers and an unflinching desire for strong, black coffee. I arrived at the river around 11 a.m. so I could fish the warmest part of the day, which is when I expected the trout to be most active. I searched for fish using midge patterns, or when I got discouraged, switched to heavily-weighted Woolly Buggers to scape the bottom. Not once did I see or feel a trout. Thoroughly cold and with fingers too stiff to change flies, I packed up and went home by three o'clock.

Then I talked to Taylor Streit and was indoctrinated into the world of winter trout fishing on the Rio Grande.

"Don't get to the river until three o'clock," Streit

the entire length of the Gorge, they are particularly heavy in the easily accessible section of river in the Bureau of Land Management's Orilla Verde Recreation Area near Pilar. After the Rio Grande's tumultuous journey through the Taos Box, the walls of the Gorge

Taos Junction Bridge in the Orilla Verde Recreation Area. Photo by S. Brooks Bedwell

Fall and winter are the best times for a fly fishing trip in the Orilla Verde Recreation area. On autumn afternoons, browns and rainbows will take nymphs or streamers fished along the bottom. Photo by Jeff Boxer

advised. "The action doesn't start until the sun dips below the canyon walls at about four, when water temperatures are highest. Start watching along the banks and in the eddies. You'll start to see the trout—big ones—quietly sipping midges in the shadows. Cast to risers. You'll rarely be successful searching for trout."

Streit has learned volumes about this tiny bug and how trout feed on them. He figures the best way to increase your chance for success is to know where the fish and bugs come together.

"Look for clear water that's not more than a couple feet deep," Streit suggests. "You won't find them feeding in still water or fast currents, but somewhere in between." At times the best way to locate feeding fish is to drive up and down the road in your car until you see rises.

"I usually fish the hatch with a size 18 or 20 midge," Streit says. He finds the specific pattern unimportant. A Griffith's Gnat or his own Snowfly, with a black thread body, quill wings, and sparse grizzly hackle, will do just fine.

When conditions are right, the trout feed almost exclusively on mating clusters. Groups of up to a dozen insects gather into floating gray orgies and the size of the clusters attract trout. Simple midge cluster patterns, not much more than black thread bodies and grizzly hackle, are the best way to take advantage of this behavior.

Successful fishing is likely to be crammed into a short window each day. The bulk of winter feeding by trout is on midges, so there is not much nymphing action. After the sun drops behind the canyon walls, you have about forty-five minutes to spot rising trout and cast to them. Not every day produces a good rise. Perfect conditions are so tenuous that the hatch takes on a mystical quality.

The cold air and water of the Gorge in winter demands caution. Neoprene chest waders are a must, supplemented with a thick fleece jacket, thermal underwear and heavy socks. A windbreaker, wool hat, and neoprene gloves help ward off the chilly air. In case of a fall, always have an extra set of dry clothes in your car.

The lower Gorge holds large numbers of stocked rainbows ranging from 6 to 16 inches. Wild browns

Wild brown trout are found throughout the Rio Grande Gorge, even in the heavily-fished stretches near Pilar.

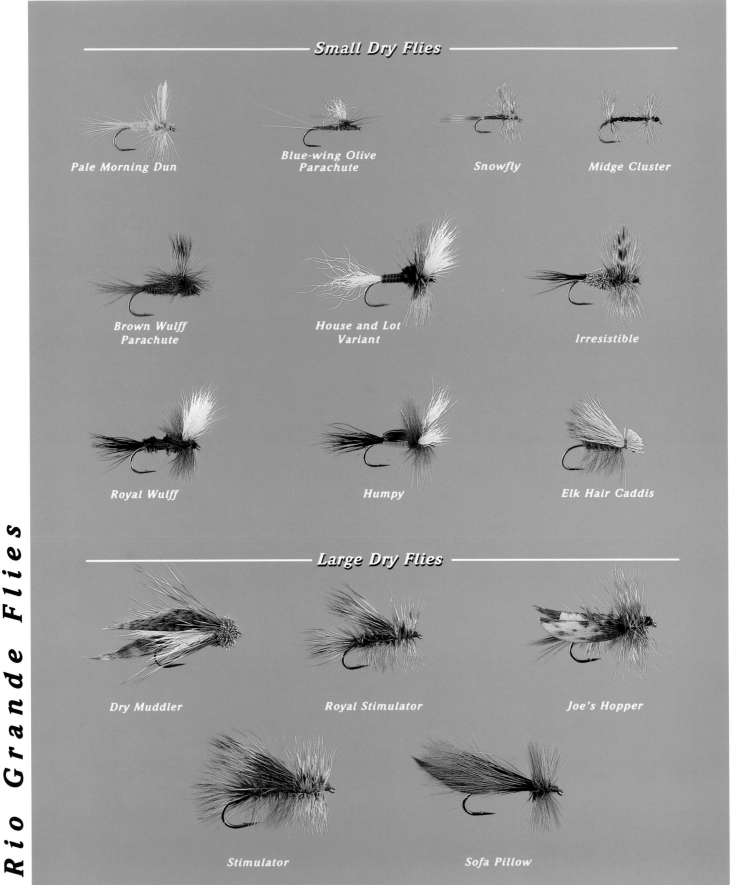

Rio Grande Flies

Small Dry Flies

Pale Morning Dun

Blue-wing Olive Parachute

Snowfly

Midge Cluster

Brown Wulff Parachute

House and Lot Variant

Irresistible

Royal Wulff

Humpy

Elk Hair Caddis

Large Dry Flies

Dry Muddler

Royal Stimulator

Joe's Hopper

Stimulator

Sofa Pillow

Nymphs

Bead Head Hare's Ear

Bead Head Prince Nymph

Pheasant Tail

Double Hackle Peacock

Poundmeister

Woven Stonefly

Cranefly Larva

Streamers

Brown and Yellow Bucktail

Brown Marabou Muddler

Dave's Crayfish

Black Woolly Bugger

Flies tied by Chris Duffy of Santa Fe, New Mexico. Additional flies by Bill Orr and Craig Martin.

A dusting of snow covers the canyon of the Rio Grande and Otowi Mesa. Photo by Craig Martin

continue to hold their own with many fish in the 12- to 14-inch range. This section is hit hard by anglers and finding larger fish is rare.

In contrast to the difficult access above, the Rio Grande south of Taos Junction Bridge is paralleled by highways. Easy access keeps the Orilla Verde Recreation Area popular throughout the year. Reach the area by turning west on State Road 570 at Pilar, twenty miles south of Taos and twenty miles north of Española on NM 68. It's a mile from Pilar to Orilla Verde where the BLM charges a small fee for day-use. The only river-level campgrounds in the Gorge are located here.

Below Pilar the Rio Grande flows through a foaming stretch of pocket water called the Racecourse, known more for its challenging whitewater rafting than its angling. Even with easy access from Highway 68, this final stretch of the Gorge sees little angling pressure. Decent-sized trout are present in small numbers south to the village of Velarde and strays are reportedly caught as far south as White Rock Canyon near Santa Fe.

The finest fly fishing rivers offer a wide diversity of angling experience, with every reach seeming like a distinct smaller stream. The Rio Grande's scenic headwaters, rugged canyons, and broad, floatable stretches hold up well against other rivers widely accepted as premier angling destinations. Although it remains a well-kept secret, the Rio Grande offers all the features of the best streams in the West.

One disadvantage of being an unknown river is that few people stand up for the Rio Grande to protect it against abuses from agricultural water use, mining, and angling pressure. Precious little research has been done on the river and its insects and fish, and even the New Mexico Department of Game and Fish fails to appreciate the high quality of the fishery in the Gorge. The Rio Grande needs more friends who are willing to speak up for it and its trout.

As the sport of fly fishing becomes more popular, it is increasingly difficult to find a stretch of river to call your own, if only for a few hours. The beauty of the Rio Grande, both in the San Juans and in the Gorge, lies in its endless, uncrowded miles of trout habitat.

Although short stretches of the river receive heavy use, it is unlikely that the headwaters or the canyons of the Rio Grande will ever see more than a few fishermen. Anglers who are looking for the opportunity to experience a forgotten type of fly fishing owe it to themselves to give the Rio Grande a try.

Further Reading

DeVries, Ralph and Stephen Mauer, Wild and Scenic Rio Grande: Lobatos Bridge to Velarde. Albuquerque: Southwest Natural and Cultural Heritage Association, 1994.

Fergusson, Erna. New Mexico, A Pageant of Three Peoples. Albuquerque: University of New Mexico Press, 1973.

Gilpin, Laura. Rio Grande: River of Destiny. New York: Duell, Sloan, and Pearce, 1949.

Horgan, Paul. The Great River. New York: Holt, Rinehart, and Winston, 1954.

Martin, Craig, ed. Fly Fishing in Northern New Mexico. Albuquerque: University of New Mexico Press, 1991.

Martin, Craig, Tom Knopick and John Flick. Fly Fishing Southern Colorado: An Angler's Guide. Boulder: Pruett Publishing, 1997.

Nichols, John. The Last Beautiful Days of Autumn. New York: Holt, Rinehart, and Winston, 1982.

For More Information

Creede-Mineral County Chamber of Commerce, P.O. Box 580, Creede, CO 81130, (719)658-2374, (800)327-2102.

New Mexico Tourism Department, 491 Old Santa Fe Trail, Santa Fe, NM 87501, (800)545-2040.

Santa Fe Convention and Visitors Bureau, P.O Box 909, Santa Fe, NM 87501, (505)984-6760, (800)777-2489.

South Fork Chamber of Commerce, P.O. Box 312, South Fork, CO 81154, (719)873-5512.

Taos County Chamber of Commerce, P.O. Drawer 1, Taos, NM 87571, (505)758-3873, (800)732-8267.

Colorado Division of Wildlife, 722 South County Road 1 East, Monte Vista, CO 81144, (719)852-4783.

Duranglers Flies and Supplies, 801B Main Avenue, Durango, CO 81301, (970)385-4081.

Gunnison River Expeditions, P.O. Box 315, Montrose, CO 81402, (970)249-4441, (800)297-4441.

High Desert Angler, 435 S. Guadalupe, Santa Fe, NM 87501, (505)988-7688.

Los Rios Anglers, P.O. Box 4006, Taos, NM 87571, (505)758-2798.

Rod Wintz Guide Service, Wason Ranch, Box 220, Creede, CO 81130, (719)658-2413.

The Solitary Angler, P.O. Box 4006, Taos, NM 87571, (505)776-5585, (800)748-1707.

Taylor Streit Fly Fishing, P.O. Box 2759, Taos, NM 87571, (505)751-1312.

Sources on the Internet

Rocky Mountain Fly Fishing Center
http://www.xmission.com/~gastown/flyfishing/index.html

The Reel Life Homepage
http://www.thereellife.com/rcellife/

New Mexico Department of Game and Fish
http://gmfish.state.nm.us

Taos Virtual Vacation Guide
http://taosweb.com/nmusa/TAOS

New Mexico Tourism
http://www.nets.com/newmextourism

Santa Fe Tourism
http://nets.com/santafe.html

Monk's Hood. Photo by Craig Martin

Ruins of Tyuonyi Pueblo in Frijoles Canyon, a tributary of the Rio Grande. Photo by Craig Martin